A GIFT FOR:
FROM:

MOCHA with MAX

friendly thoughts & simple truths
from the writings of...

MAX
Lucado

J. COUNTRYMAN • NASHVILLE, TENNESSEE

Published by J. Countryman, a division of Thomas Nelson, Inc, Nashville, Tennessee 37214.

Compiled and edited by Terri Gibbs

Editorial Supervision: Karen Hill, Administrative Editor for Max Lucado

Designed by The DesignWorks Group, www.thedesignworksgroup.com

www.thomasnelson.com
www.jcountryman.com

ISBN:1-40410-095-4

Printed and bound in the United States of America

CONTENTS

P R E F A C E

Need a word of encouragement? Looking for a funny story? Wondering what's happening in people's lives? In our office, everyone knows there's one place to go: the coffee pot in the staff kitchen.

Throughout the day, you'll find secretaries, ministers, youth interns, and maintenance workers milling around the "filling station." We all gather for more than just a cup of caffeine . . . we're thirsty for a cup of fellowship.

I pray this little book will lead you to some satisfying moments of fellowship with the Father.

Pull up a chair. Turn off all the things that beep and beckon.

Drink deeply, linger awhile. Have a cup on me!

Max

SECTION ONE

Let's talk about you for a minute . . .

Coffee
Don't for a microsecond think
this you. Washing
enough him. He place
the Better stated, he places

God is for you. Your parents may have forgotten you, your teachers may have neglected you, your siblings may be ashamed of you; but within reach of your prayers is the maker of the oceans, God!

God is for you. Not "may be," not "has been," not "was," not "would be," but "God is!" He is for you. Today. At this hour. At this minute. No need to wait in line or come back tomorrow. He is with you. He could not be closer than he is at this second. His loyalty won't increase if you are better nor lessen if you are worse. He is for you.

Can your purpose be taken or your value diminished? No.

No one can defeat you.

God is for you.

In the Grip of Grace

God Loves you simply because he has chosen to do so.

He loves you when you don't feel lovely.

He loves you when no one else loves you. Others may abandon you, divorce you, and ignore you, but God will love you. Always. No matter what.

A Love Worth Giving

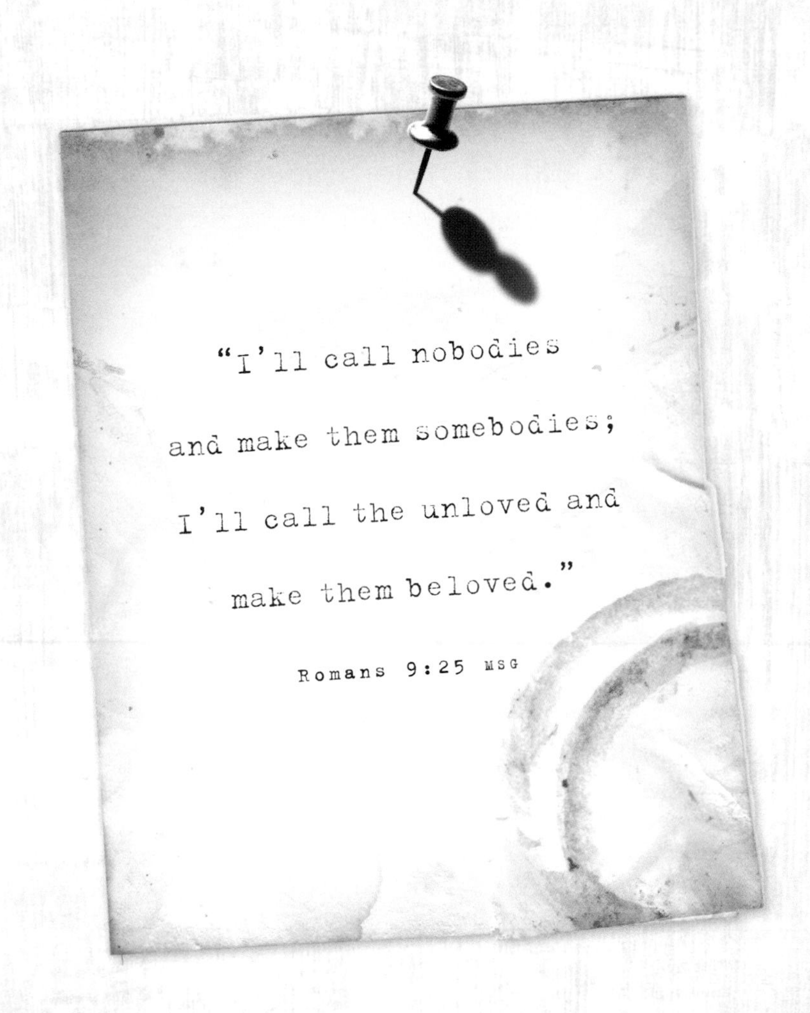
"I'll call nobodies
and make them somebodies;
I'll call the unloved and
make them beloved."
Romans 9:25 MSG

YOU'RE WORTH GOD'S KINDNESS

In the book titled *Sweet Thursday,* John Steinbeck introduces us to Madam Fauna. She runs a brothel and takes a liking to a prostitute by the name of Suzy. Madam Fauna sets Suzy up on a real date with a man, not a client. She buys Suzy a nice dress and helps her get ready for the evening. As Suzy is leaving, she, moved by Madam Fauna's kindness, asks her, "You have done so much for me. Can I do anything for you?"

"Yes," the older woman replies, "you can say, 'I'm Suzy and no one else.'"

Suzy does. Then Madam Fauna requests, "Now say, 'I'm Suzy, and I'm a good thing.'"

And so Suzy tries. "I'm Suzy, and I'm a good …" And Suzy begins to cry.

Wouldn't God want you to say the same words? In his book you are a *good thing.* Be kind to yourself. God thinks you're worth his kindness. And he's a good judge of character.

A Love Worth Giving

Birmingham
Dec. 16-19
Dear Amanda:
Well, after much
wandering around, I
am, again, at h
Arrived

Mrs. Amanda Sutton
Mt. Pleasant
Tennessee

God loves you.

Personally. Powerfully.

Passionately.

others have promised and failed.

But God has promised and succeeded.

He loves you

with an unfailing love.

GOD ON THE INSIDE

In high school my brother and I shared a '65 Rambler station wagon. The clunker had as much glamour as Forrest Gump: three speed, shift on the column, bench seats covered with plastic, no air conditioning.

And, oh, the engine. Our lawn mower had more power. The car's highest speed, downhill with a tailwind, was fifty miles per hour. To this day I'm convinced that my father (a trained mechanic) searched for the slowest possible car and bought it for us.

When we complained about her pitiful shape, he just smiled and said, "Fix it up." We did the best we could. We cleaned the carpets, sprayed air freshener on the seats, stuck a peace symbol on the back window, and hung dice from the rearview mirror. We removed the hubcaps and spray-painted the rims black. The car looked better, smelled better, but ran the same. Still a clunker—a clean clunker, to be sure—but still a clunker.

Don't for a microsecond think God does this with you. Washing the outside isn't enough for him. He places power on the inside. Better stated, he places *himself* on the inside.

Next Door Savior

"Fix it up."

You knit me
together in my mother's womb.

psalm 139:13, NIV

Think on those words. You were knitted together. You aren't an accident. You weren't mass-produced. You aren't an assembly-line product. You were deliberately planned, specifically gifted, and lovingly positioned on this earth by the Master Craftsman.

In a society that has little room for second fiddles, that's good news. In a culture where the door of opportunity opens only once and then slams shut, that is a revelation. In a system that ranks the value of a human by the figures of his salary or the shape of her legs . . . let me tell you something: this is a reason for joy!

The Applause of Heaven

God views your life the way you view
a movie after you've read the boo
When something bad happens, yo
feel the air suck ... the theater.
Ev... one ... crisis on
the screen. ... You've
read the book. You know how the
good ... s out of the tight spot.

God views your life the way you view a movie after you've read the book. When something bad happens, you feel the air sucked out of the theater. Everyone else gasps at the crisis on the screen. Not you. Why? You've read the book. You know how the good guy gets out of the tight spot. God views your life with the same confidence. He's not only read your story . . . he wrote it. His perspective is different, and his purpose is clear.

Come Thirsty

"I know the plans I have for you," declares the Lord, "plans to prosper you and not to harm you, plans to give you hope and a future."

Jeremiah 29:11, NIV

your place in heaven

was more important to Christ

than his place in heaven,

so he gave up his

so you could have yours.

SECTION TWO

what's life without JOY and MUSIC?

Never outgrow your love of sunsets.

Bedtime is a bad time for kids. No child understands the logic of going to bed while there is energy left in the body or hours left in the day.

My children are no exception. A few years ago, after many objections and countless groans, the girls were finally in their gowns, in their beds, and on their pillows. I slipped into the room to give them a final kiss. Andrea, the five-year-old was still awake, just barely, but awake. After I kissed her, she lifted her eyelids one final time and said, "I can't wait until I wake up."

Oh, for the attitude of a five-year-old! That simple uncluttered passion for living that can't wait for tomorrow. A philosophy of life that reads, "Play hard, laugh hard, and leave the worries to your father." A bottomless well of optimism flooded by a perpetual spring of faith.

And the Angels Were Silent

It is the normality not the uniqueness of God's miracles that causes them to be so staggering. Rather than shocking the globe with an occasional demonstration of deity, God has opted to display his power daily. Proverbially. Pounding waves. Prism-cast colors. Birth, death, life. We are surrounded by miracles. God is throwing testimonies at us like fireworks, each one exploding, "God is! God is!" . . .

God Came Near

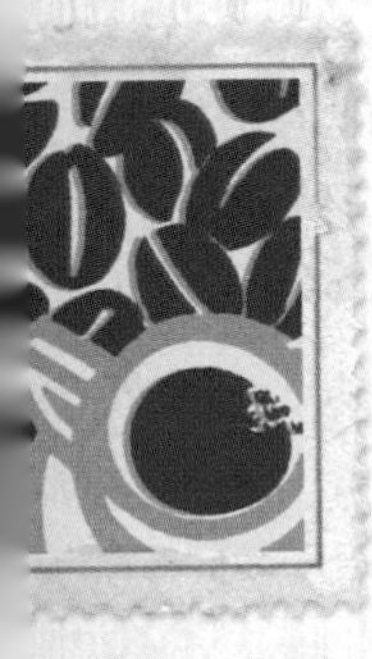

The next time
you hear a baby laugh
or see an ocean wave,
take note.
Pause and listen
as His Majesty whispers
ever so gently,
"I'm here."

caffe
Coffee

God wants you to hear his music.

He has a rhythm that will race your heart and lyrics that will stir your tears. You want to journey to the stars? He can take you there. You want to lie down in peace? His music can soothe your soul.

But first, he's got to get rid of that country-western stuff. (Forgive me, Nashville. Only an example.)

And so he begins tossing the CDs. A friend turns away. The job goes bad. Your spouse doesn't understand. The church is dull. One by one he removes the options until all you have left is God.

He would do that? Absolutely. "The Lord disciplines those he loves" (Heb. 12:6). If he must silence every voice, he will. He wants you to hear his music. He wants you to discover what David discovered and to be able to say what David said.

"You are with me."

Yes, you, Lord, are in heaven. Yes, you rule the universe. Yes, you sit upon the stars and make your home in the deep. But yes, yes, yes, you are with me.

The Lord is with me.

Traveling Light

"Cut loose."

WANT TO CHANGE THE WAY YOU SING?

As we behold Christ, we become like him.

I experienced this principle firsthand when an opera singer visited our church. We didn't know his voice was trained. You couldn't have known by his corduroy coat and loafers. No tuxedo, cummerbund, or silk tie. His appearance raised no eyebrow, but his voice certainly did. I should know. He was in the pew behind mine.

His vibrato made dentures rattle and rafters shake. He tried to contain himself. But how can a tuba hide in a room of piccolos?

For a moment I was startled. But within a verse, I was inspired. Emboldened by his volume, I lifted mine. Did I sing better? Not even I could hear me. My warbles were lost in his talent. But did I try harder? No doubt. His power brought out the best in me.

Could your world use a little music? If so, invite heaven's baritone to cut loose. He may look as common as the guy next door, but just wait till you see what he can do. Who knows? A few songs with him might change the way you sing.

Forever.

Next Door Savior

Love, joy, peace, patience, kindness, goodness, faithfulness, gentleness, and self-control. To these I commit my day. If I succeed, I will give thanks. If I fail, I will seek his grace. And then, when this day is done, I will place my head on my pillow and rest.

eternal instants. You've had them. We all have.

Sharing a porch swing on a summer evening with your grandchild.

Seeing her face in the glow of a candle.

Putting your arm into your husband's as you stroll through the golden leaves and breathe the brisk autumn air.

Listening to your six-year-old thank God for everything from goldfish to Grandma.

Such moments are necessary because they remind us that everything is okay. The King is still on the throne and life is still worth living. Eternal instants remind us that love is still the greatest possession and the future is nothing to fear.

The next time an instant in your life begins to be eternal, let it.

God Came Near

God will load your world

with flowers.

He hand-delivers a bouquet to your door

every day.

Open it! Take them!

Within an hour I'll be in Denalyn's kitchen sniffing the dinner trimmings like a Labrador sniffing for wild game. When she's not looking, I'll snatch a foretaste. Just a bite of turkey, a spoon of chili, a corner of bread . . . predinner snacks stir appetites for the table.

Samplings from heaven's kitchen do likewise. There are moments, perhaps far too few, when time evaporates and joy modulates and heaven hands you an hors d'oeuvre.

- Your newborn has passed from restlessness to rest. Beneath the amber light of a midnight moon, you trace a soft finger across tiny, sleeping eyes and wonder, *God gave you to me?* A prelibation from heaven's winery.

- You're lost in the work you love to do, were made to do. As you step back from the moist canvas or hoed garden or rebuilt V-eight engine,

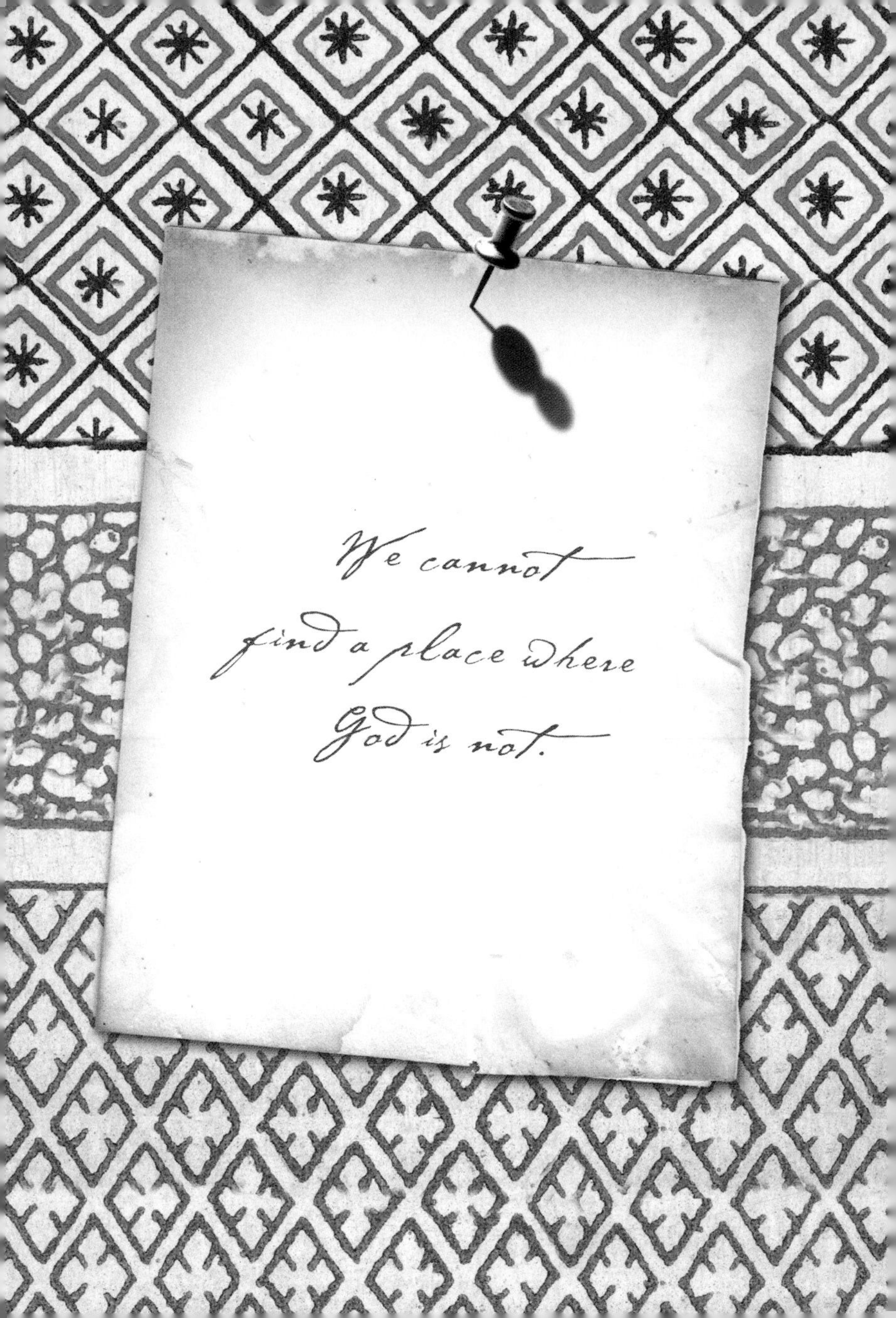
We cannot
find a place where
God is not.

satisfaction flows within like a gulp of cool water, and the angel asks, "Another apéritif?"

- The lyrics to the hymn say what you couldn't but wanted to, and for a moment, a splendid moment, there are no wars, wounds, or tax returns. Just you, God, and a silent assurance that everything is right with the world.

come Thirsty

SECTION THREE

what's LOVE got to do with it?

God's Love changed the woman in Samaria.

Talk about a woman who could make a list of wrongs. Number one, discrimination. She is a Samaritan, hated by Jews. Number two, gender bias. She is a female, condescended to by the men. Third, she is a divorcée, not once, not twice. Let's see if we can count. Four? Five? Five marriages turned south, and now she's sharing a bed with a guy who won't give her a ring.

When I add this up, I envision a happy-hour stool sitter who lives with her mad at half boil. Husky voice, cigarette breath, and a dress cut low at the top and high at the bottom. Certainly not

Samaria's finest. Certainly not the woman you'd put in charge of the Ladies' Bible class.

Which makes the fact that Jesus does just that all the more surprising. He doesn't just put her in charge of the class; he puts her in charge of evangelizing the whole town. Before the day is over, the entire city hears about a man who claims to be God. "He told me everything I ever did" (John 4:39), she tells them, leaving unsaid the obvious, "and he loved me anyway."

A little rain can straighten a flower stem. A little love can change a life.

A Love Worth Giving

others love you because of you, because your dimples dip when you smile or your rhetoric charms when you flirt. Some people love you because of you. Not God. He loves you because he is he. He loves you because he decides to. Self-generated, uncaused, and spontaneous, his constant-level love depends on his choice to give it.

A Love Worth Giving

God offers authentic love.
His devotion is the real deal.
But he won't give you the genuine
until you surrender the imitations.

Perfect love is just that—perfect, a perfect knowledge of the past and a perfect vision of the future. You cannot shock God with your actions. There will never be a day that you cause him to gasp, "Whoa, did you see what she just did?" Never will he turn to his angels and bemoan, "Had I known Max was going to go Spam-brained on me, I wouldn't have saved his soul." God knows your entire story, from first word to final breath, and with clear assessment declares, "You are mine."

My publisher made a similar decision with this book. Before agreeing to publish it, they read it—every single word. Multiple sets of editorial eyes scoured the manuscript, moaning at my bad jokes, grading my word crafting, suggesting a tune-up here and a tone-down there. We volleyed pages back and forth, writer to editor to writer, until finally we all agreed—this is it. It's time to publish or pass. The publisher could pass, mind you. Sometimes they do.

But in this case, obviously they didn't. With perfect knowledge of this imperfect product, they signed on. What you read may surprise you, but not them.

What you do may stun you, but not God. With perfect knowledge of your imperfect life, God signed on.

come Thirsty

Such love has no fear
because perfect love expels all fear.
If we are afraid, it is for fear of judgment,
and this shows that his love has not been
perfected in us. (1 John 4:17–18, NLT)

We all need improvement, but we don't need to woo God's love. We change because we already have God's love.

God's *perfect* love.

GOD LOVES TO BE WITH THE ONES HE LOVES

A family of black-tailed squirrels has made its home amid the roots of the tree north of my office. We've been neighbors for three years now. They watch me peck the keyboard. I watch them store their nuts and climb the trunk. We're mutually amused. I could watch them all day. Sometimes I do.

But I've never considered becoming one of them. The squirrel world holds no appeal to me. Who wants to sleep next to a hairy rodent with beady eyes? (No comments from you wives who feel you already do.) Give up the Rocky Mountains, bass fishing, weddings, and laughter for a hole in the ground and a diet of dirty nuts? Count me out.

But count Jesus in. What a world he left. Our classiest mansion would be a tree trunk to him. Earth's finest cuisine would be walnuts on heaven's table. And the idea of becoming a squirrel with claws and tiny teeth and a furry tail? It's nothing compared to God becoming a one-celled embryo and entering the womb of Mary.

But he did. The God of the universe kicked against the wall of a womb, was born into the poverty of a peasant, and spent his first night in the feed-trough of a cow.

Why? He loves to be with the ones he loves.

Next Door Savior

POST CARD
THIS SIDE FOR THE ADDRESS
This is love:
not that we loved God,
but that he loved us.
1 John 4:10, NIV

Love . . . endures all things.

1 Corinthians 13:4–7, NKJV

Love goes the distance . . . and Christ traveled from limitless eternity to be confined by time in order to become one of us. He didn't have to. He could have given up. At any step along the way he could have called it quits.

When he saw the size of the womb, he could have stopped.

When he saw how tiny his hand would be, how soft his voice would be, how hungry his tummy would be, he could have stopped. At the first whiff of the stinky stable, at the first gust of cold air. The first time he scraped his knee or blew his nose or tasted burnt bagels, he could have turned and walked out.

When he saw the dirt floor of his Nazareth house. When Joseph gave him a chore to do. When his fellow students were dozing off during the reading of the Torah, his Torah. When the neighbor took his name in vain. When the lazy farmer blamed his poor crop on God. At any point Jesus could have said, "That's it! That's enough! I'm going home." But he didn't.

He didn't, because he is love.

A Love Worth Giving

LOVE LIKE A CAFETERIA LINE?

My parents were not too big on restaurants. Partly because of the selection in our small town. Dairy Queen offered the gourmet selection, and everything went downhill from there. The main reason, though, was practicality. Why eat out when you can stay home? Restaurant trips were a Sunday-only, once-or-twice-a-month event. We typically ate at home. And every time we ate at home, my mom gave my brother and me the same instructions: "Put a little bit of everything on your plate."

We never had to be told to clean the plate. Eating volume was not a challenge. Variety was. Don't get me wrong, Mom was a good cook. But boiled okra? Asparagus? More like "croak-ra" and "gasp-aragus." Were they really intended for human consumption?

According to Mom, they were, and—according to Mom—they had to be eaten. "Eat some of everything." That was the rule in our house.

But that was not the rule at the cafeteria. On special occasions we made the forty-five-minute drive to the greatest culinary innovation since the gas stove: the cafeteria line. Ah, what a fine moment indeed to take a tray and gaze down the midway at the endless options. A veritable cornucopia of fine cuisine. Down the row you walk, intoxicated by the selection and liberated by the freedom. Yes to the fried fish; no to the fried tomatoes. Yes to the pecan pie; no, no, a thousand times no to the "croak-ra" and "gasp-aragus." Cafeteria lines are great.

Wouldn't it be nice if love were like a cafeteria line? What if you could look at the person with whom you live and select what you want and pass on what you don't? What if parents could do this with kids? "I'll take a plate of good grades and cute smiles, and I'm passing on the teenage identity crisis and tuition bills."

What if kids could do the same with parents? "Please give me a helping of allowances and free lodging but no rules or curfews, thank you."

And spouse with spouse? "H'm, how about a bowl of good health and good moods. But job transfers, in-laws, and laundry are not on my diet."

Wouldn't it be great if love were like a cafeteria line? It would be easier. It would be neater. It would be painless and peaceful. But you know what? It wouldn't be love. Love doesn't accept just a few things. Love is willing to accept all things.

God's view of love is like my mom's view of food. When we love someone, we take the entire package. No picking and choosing. No large helpings of the good and passing on the bad. Love is a package deal.

A Love Worth Giving

WHAT IS LOVE?

Love is patient, love is kind.
It does not envy, it does not boast, it is not proud.
It is not rude, it is not self-seeking, it is not easily angered, it keeps no record of wrongs.
Love does not delight in evil but rejoices with the truth.
It always protects, always trusts, always hopes, always perseveres. Love never fails.

1 Corinthians 13: 4-8, NIV

Several years ago someone challenged me to replace the word *love* in this passage with my name. I did and became a liar. "Max is patient, Max is kind. Max does not envy, he does not boast, he is not proud. . . ." That's enough! Stop right there! Those words are false. Max is not patient. Max is not kind. Ask my wife and kids. Max can be an out-and-out clod! That's my problem.

Love . . .

bears all things,

believes all things,

hopes all things,

endures all things.

And for years that was my problem with this paragraph. It set a standard I could not meet. No one can meet it. No one, that is, except Christ. Does this passage not describe the measureless love of God? Let's insert Christ's name in place of the word *love,* and see if it rings true.

Jesus is patient, Jesus is kind. Jesus does not envy, he does not boast, he is not proud. Jesus is not rude, he is not self-seeking, he is not easily angered, he keeps no record of wrongs. Jesus does not delight in evil but rejoices with the truth. Jesus always protects, always trusts, always hopes, always perseveres. Jesus never fails.

Rather than let this scripture remind us of a love we cannot produce, let it remind us of a love we cannot resist—God's love.

A Love Worth Giving

You want to plumb the depths

of your love for someone?

Love never celebrates misfortune.

Never.

LOVE NEVER CELEBRATES MISFORTUNE

The summer before my eighth-grade year I made friends with a guy named Larry. He was new to town, so I encouraged him to go out for our school football team. He could meet some guys, and being a stocky fellow, he might even make the squad. He agreed.

The result was a good news—bad news scenario. The good news? He made the cut. The bad news? He won my position. I was demoted to second string. I tried to be happy for him, but it was tough.

A few weeks into the season Larry fell off a motorcycle and broke a finger. I remember the day he stood at my front door holding up his bandaged hand. "Looks like you're going to have to play."

I tried to feel sorry for him, but it was hard. The passage was a lot easier for Paul to write than it was for me to practice. "Rejoice with those who rejoice, and weep with those who weep" (Rom. 12:15, NASB).

Does God love us because of our goodness? Because of our kindness? Because of our great faith?

No, he loves us because of *his* goodness, kindness, and great faith. Isn't it good to know that even when we don't love with a perfect love, God does?

A Love Worth Giving

SECTION FOUR

can I speak candidly about PATIENCE and ENDURANCE?

For some of you, the journey has been long. Very long and stormy. Some of you have shouldered burdens that few of us could ever carry. You have bid farewell to life-long partners. You have been robbed of life-long dreams. You have been given bodies that can't sustain your spirit. You have spouses who can't tolerate your faith. You have bills that outnumber the paychecks and challenges that outweigh the strength.

And you are tired.

It's hard for you to see the City in the midst of the storms. The desire to pull over to the side of the road and get out entices you. You want to go on, but some days the road seems so long.

Let me encourage you. God never said that the

journey would be easy, but he did say that the arrival would be worthwhile.

Remember this: God may not do what you want, but he will do what is right . . . and best. He's the Father of forward motion. Trust him. He will get you home. And the trials of the trip will be lost in the joys of the feast.

In the Eye of the Storm

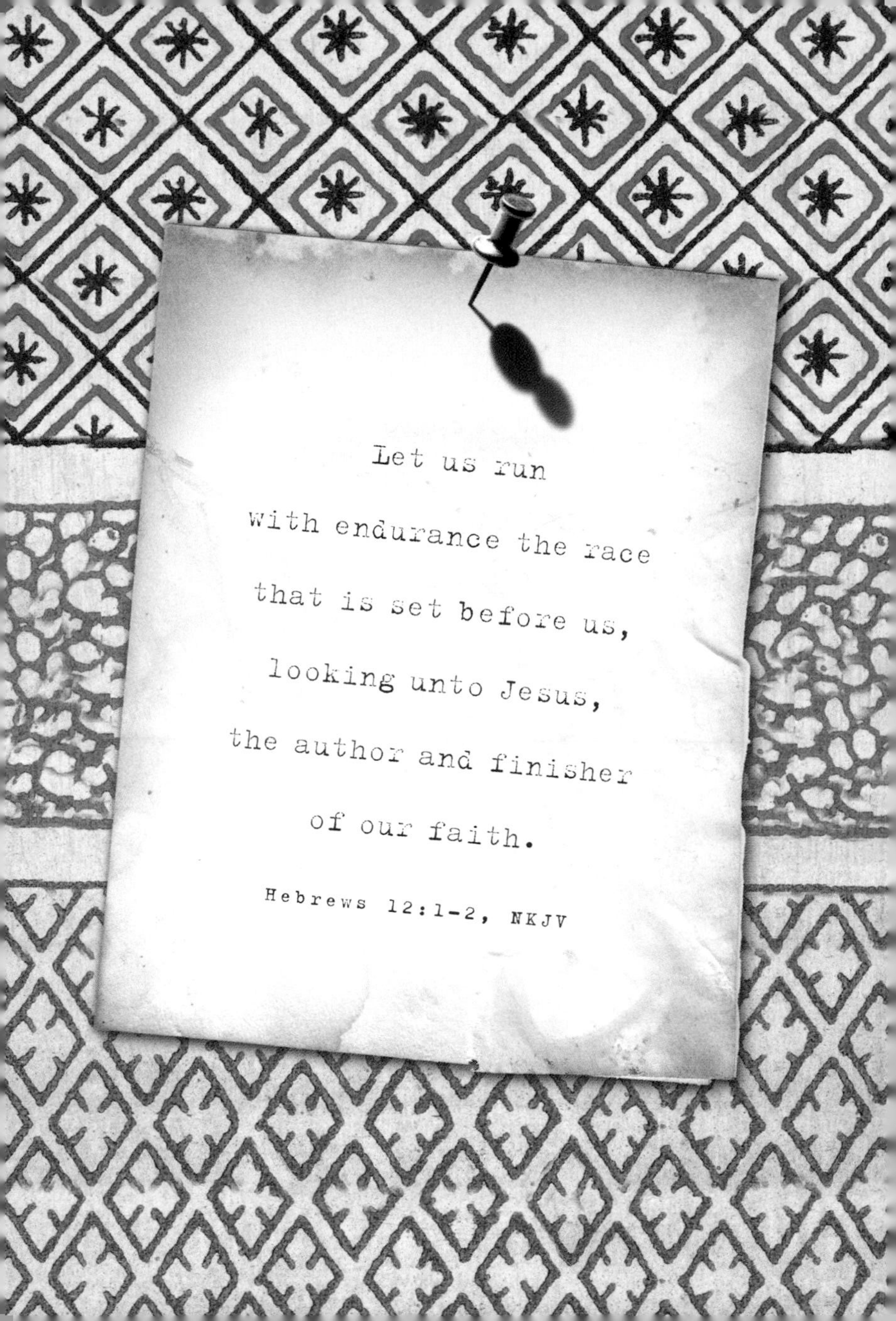
Let us run
with endurance the race
that is set before us,
looking unto Jesus,
the author and finisher
of our faith.
Hebrews 12:1-2, NKJV

FIX YOUR EYES ON THE SON

I'm a runner. More mornings than not I drag myself out of bed and onto the street. I don't run fast. And compared to marathoners, I don't run far. But I run. I run because I don't like cardiologists.

Since heart disease runs in our family, I run in our neighborhood. As the sun is rising, I am running. And as I am running, my body is groaning. It doesn't want to cooperate. My knee hurts. My hip is stiff. My ankles complain. Sometimes a passerby laughs at my legs, and my ego hurts.

Things hurt. And as things hurt, I've learned that I have three options. Go home. (Denalyn would laugh at me.) Meditate on my hurts until I start imagining I'm having chest pains. (Pleasant thought.) Or I can keep running and watch the sun come up. My trail has just enough easterly bend to give me a front-row seat for God's morning miracle. If I watch God's world go from dark to golden, guess what? The same happens to my attitude. The pain passes and the joints loosen, and before I know it, the run is half over and life ain't half bad. Everything improves as I fix my eyes on the sun.

Traveling Light

Patience is a fruit of God's Spirit. It hangs from the tree of Galatians 5:22 (NCV): *"The Spirit produces the fruit of love, joy, peace, patience."*

one of God's cures for weak faith? A good, healthy struggle. Several years ago our family visited Colonial Williamsburg, a re-creation of eighteenth-century America in Williamsburg, Virginia. If you ever visit there, pay special attention to the work of the silversmith. The craftsman places an ingot of silver on an anvil and pounds it with a sledgehammer. Once the metal is flat enough for shaping, into the furnace it goes. The worker alternately heats and pounds the metal until it takes the shape of a tool he can use.

Heating, pounding.
Heating, pounding.
Deadlines, traffic.
Arguments, disrespect.
Loud sirens, silent phones.
Heating, pounding.
Heating, pounding.

Did you know that the *smith* in *silversmith* comes from the old English word *smite?* Silversmiths are accomplished smiters. So is God. Once the worker is satisfied with the form of his tool, he begins to planish and pumice it. Using smaller hammers and abrasive pads, he taps, rubs, and decorates. And no one stops him. No one yanks the hammer out of his hand and says, "Go easy on that silver. You've pounded enough!" No, the craftsman buffets the metal until he is finished with it. Some silversmiths, I'm told, keep polishing until they can see their face in the tool. When will God stop with you? When he sees his reflection in you.

come Thirsty

ever feel as if you need to get away? So did Jesus.

"Early the next morning, while it was still dark, Jesus woke and left the house. He went to a lonely place, where he prayed" (Mark 1:35, NCV).

Ever have so many demands that you can't stop for lunch? He can relate.

"Crowds of people were coming and going so that Jesus and his followers did not even have time to eat" (Mark 6:31, NCV).

Do you have too much e-mail to fit in a screen or too many calls to make in a day? Christ has been there.

"Great crowds came to Jesus, bringing with them the lame, the blind, the crippled, those who could not speak, and many others. They put them at Jesus' feet, and he healed them" (Matthew 15:30, NCV).

How about family tension?

"When his family heard what was happening, they tried to take him home with them. 'He's out of his mind,' they said" (Mark 3:21, NLT).

Do your friends ever let you down? When Christ needed help, his friends dozed off.

"You men could not stay awake with me for one hour?" (Matthew 26:40, NCV).

When you turn to him *for* help, he runs to you *to* help. Why? He knows how you feel. He's been there.

Next Door Savior

Love is patient.

1 Corinthians 13:4

The Greek word used here for *patience* is a descriptive one. It figuratively means "taking a long time to boil." Think about a pot of boiling water. What factors determine the speed at which it boils? The size of the stove? No. The pot? The utensil may have an influence, but the primary factor is the intensity of the flame. Water boils quickly when the flame is high. It boils slowly when the flame is low. Patience "keeps the burner down."

Helpful clarification, don't you think? Patience isn't naive. It doesn't ignore misbehavior. It just keeps the flame low. It waits. It listens. It's slow to boil. This is how God treats us. And, according to Jesus, this is how we should treat others.

A Love Worth Giving

sometimes

the most godly thing

we can do

is take a day off.

STOP AND REST

Several years ago my daughter Andrea and I had a bicycle adventure. She had just learned to keep her balance on a two-wheeler and was ready to leave the safety of the front street and try the hill behind our house. She'd never ridden down a hill before.

We sat atop the descent and looked down it. To her it was Everest. "You sure you want to try?" I asked.

"I think so," she gulped.

"Just put on your brakes when you want to stop. Don't forget your brakes."

"Okay."

I rode my bike to the midway point and waited. Down she came. The bike began to pick up speed. The handlebars began to shake. Her eyes got big. Her pedals moved in a blur. As she raced past she screamed, "I can't remember how to stop pedaling!"

She crashed into the curb.

If you don't know how to stop, the result can be

painful. True on bikes. True in life.

We need one day in which work comes to a screeching halt. We need one twenty-four-hour period in which the wheels stop grinding and the motor stops turning. We need to stop.

and the angels were silent

SECTION FIVE
ANXIETY and STRESS.
[now there's a couple of topics for conversation.]

Don't spend
tomorrow's money
today.

worry changes nothing. You don't add one day to your life or one bit of life to your day by worrying. Your anxiety earns you heartburn, nothing more. Regarding the things about which we fret:

- 40 percent never happen
- 30 percent regard unchangeable deeds of the past
- 12 percent focus on the opinions of others that cannot be controlled
- 10 percent center on personal health, which only worsens as we worry about it
- 8 percent concern real problems that we can influence

Ninety-two percent of our worries are needless! Not only is worry irrelevant, doing nothing; worry is irreverent, distrusting God.

Worry is an option, not an assignment. God can lead you into a worry-free world. Be quick to pray. Focus less on the problems ahead and more on the victories behind. Do your part, and God will do his. He will guard your heart with his peace . . . a peace that passes understanding.

Come Thirsty

Be anxious for nothing,

but in everything by prayer

and supplication, with thanksgiving,

let your requests be made known

to God; and the peace of God,

which surpasses all understanding,

will guard your hearts and minds

through Christ Jesus.

Philippians 4:6-7 NKJV

A good memory makes for a good heart.

It works like this. Let's say a stress stirrer comes your way. The doctor decides you need an operation. She detects a lump and thinks it best that you have it removed. So there you are, walking out of her office. You've just been handed this cup of anxiety. What are you going to do with it? You can place it in one of two pots.

You can dump your bad news in the vat of worry and pull out the spoon. Turn on the fire. Stew on it. Stir it. Mope for a while. Brood for a time. Won't be long before you'll have a delightful pot of pessimism. Some of you have been sipping from this vat for a long time. Your friends and family have asked me to tell you that the stuff you're drinking is getting to you.

How about a different idea? The pot of prayer. Before the door of the doctor's office closes, give the

problem to God. "I receive your lordship. Nothing comes to me that hasn't passed through you."
In addition, stir in a healthy helping of gratitude. You don't think about a lion and bear, but you do remember the tax refund, the timely counsel, or the suddenly open seat on the overbooked flight. A glimpse into the past generates strength for the future.

Your part is prayer and gratitude. God's part? Peace and protection.

come Thirsty

"Give your entire attention
to what God is doing right now,
and don't get worked up
about what may or
may not happen tomorrow.
God will help you deal
with whatever hard things
come up when the time comes."

Matthew 6:34, MSG

Meet today's problems with today's
strength. Don't start tackling
tomorrow's problems until tomorrow.
You do not have tomorrow's strength yet.
You simply have enough for today.

ANXIOUS MOMENTS OR GOOD MOMENTS?

A man told his psychologist that his anxieties were disturbing his dreams. Some nights he dreamed he was a pup tent; other nights he dreamed he was a tepee. The doctor quickly analyzed the situation and replied, "I know your problem. You're too tense."

Most of us are. We parents have it especially tough. My daughters are at that age when they are starting to drive. It seems like just yesterday I was teaching them to walk, and now I'm putting them behind a steering wheel. It's a scary thought. I'm thinking of making a special bumper sticker for Jenna's car that reads, "How am I driving? 1-800-CALL-DAD."

What do we do with these worries? . . .

Do yourself a favor; take your anxious moments

to the cross. Leave them there with your bad moments, your mad moments, and your anxious moments. . . .

About this time someone is thinking, “You know, Max, if I leave all those moments at the cross, I won’t have any moments left but good ones.”

Well, what do you know? I guess you won’t.

HE CHOSE THE NAILS

stand and consider:

- The Hubble Space Telescope sends back infrared images of faint galaxies that are perhaps twelve billion light-years away (twelve billion times six trillion miles).

- Astronomers venture a feeble estimate that the number of stars in the universe equals the number of grains of sand on all the beaches of the world. The star Eta Carinae outshines our sun, in the same way Yankee Stadium outshines a cigarette lighter. Five million times brighter!

- The star Betelgeuse has a diameter of 100 million miles, which is larger than the earth's orbit around the sun.

Why the immensity? Why such vast, unmeasured, unexplored, "unused" space? So that you and I, freshly stunned, could be stirred by this resolve: "I can do all things through Christ who strengthens me" (Philippians 4:13, NKJV).

The Christ of the galaxies is the Christ of your Mondays. The Starmaker manages your travel schedule. Relax. You have a friend in high places.

Next Door Savior

God isn't going to
let you see the distant scene.
So you might as well quit looking for it.
He promises a lamp unto our feet,
not a crystal ball into the future.
We do not need to know what
will happen tomorrow.
We only need to know He leads.

Traveling Light

"That was me."

LEAVE YOUR ANGER AT THE TREE

Many years ago a stressful job stirred within T. D. Terry daily bouts of anger. His daughter, upon hearing him describe them years later, responded with surprise. "I don't remember any anger during those years."

He asked if she remembered the tree—the one near the driveway about halfway between the gate and the house. "Remember how it used to be tall? Then lost a few limbs? And after some time was nothing more than a stump?"

She did.

"That was me," T. D. explained. "I took my anger out on the tree. I kicked it. I took an ax to it. I tore the limbs. I didn't want to come home mad, so I left my anger at the tree."*

Let's do the same. In fact, let's go a step farther. Rather than take out our anger on a tree in the yard, let's take our anger to the tree on the hill. Leave your anger at the tree of Calvary. When others reject you, let God accept you. He is not frowning. He is not mad. He sings over you. Take a long drink from his limitless love, and cool down.

A Love Worth Giving

(*Roger Emmit, *Anger Management*)

SECTION SIX

what's your definition of HOPE?

Hope is not what you expect; it is what you would never dream. It is a wild, improbable tale with a pinch-me-I'm-dreaming ending. It's Abraham adjusting his bifocals so he can see not his grandson, but his son. It's Moses standing in the promised land not with Aaron or Miriam at his side, but with Elijah and the transfigured Christ. It's Zechariah left speechless at the sight of his wife Elizabeth, gray-headed and pregnant. And it is the two Emmaus-bound pilgrims reaching out to take a piece of bread only to see that the hands from which it is offered are pierced.

Hope is not a granted wish or a favor performed; no, it is far greater than that. It is a zany, unpredictable dependence on a God who loves to surprise us out of our socks and be there in the flesh to see our reaction.

God Came Near

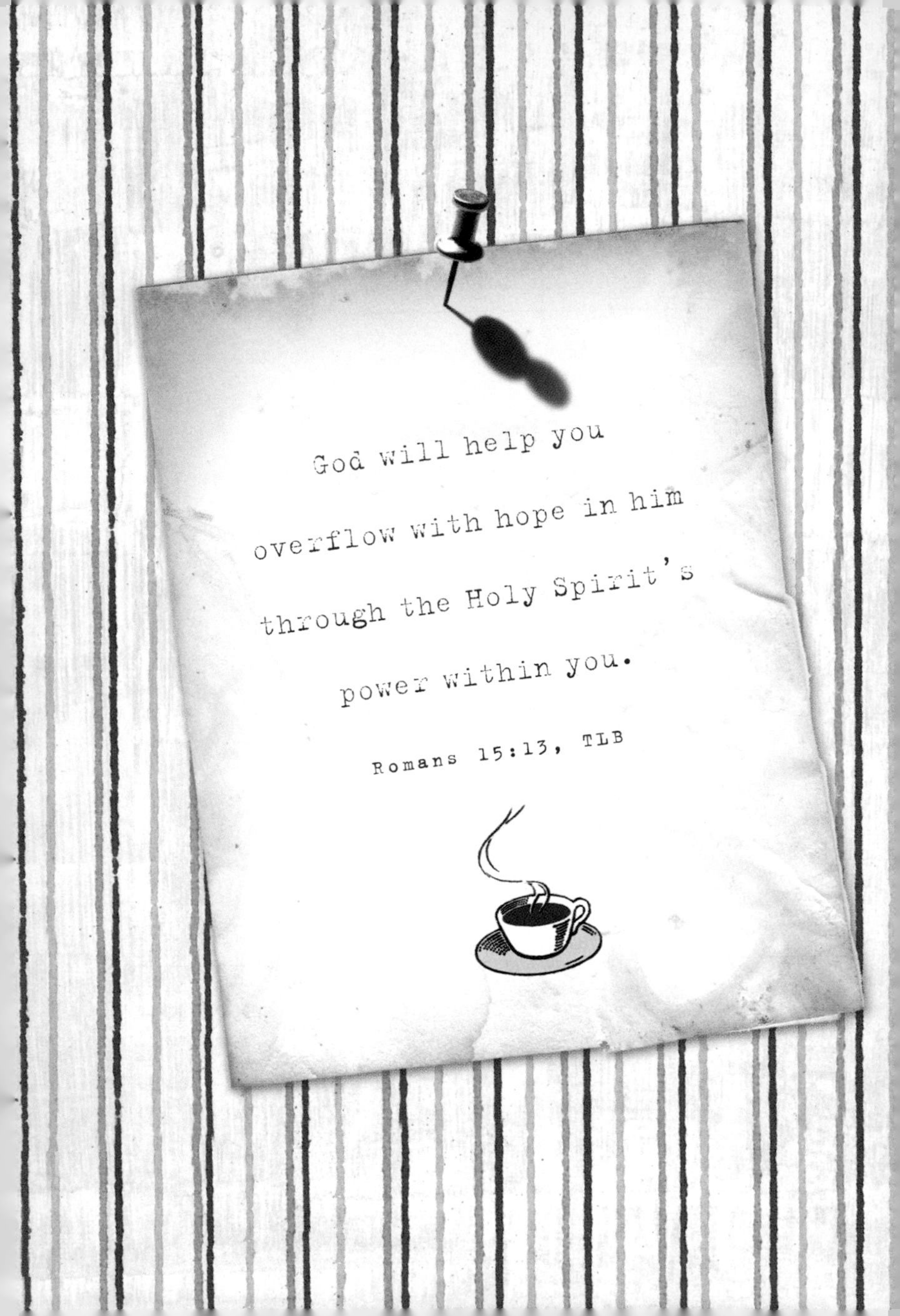
God will help you
overflow with hope in him
through the Holy Spirit's
power within you.
Romans 15:13, TLB

Heaven's hope does for your world what the sunlight did for my grandmother's cellar. I owe my love of peach preserves to her. She canned her own and stored them in an underground cellar near her West Texas house. It was a deep hole with wooden steps, plywood walls, and a musty smell. As a youngster I used to climb in, close the door, and see how long I could last in the darkness. Not even a slit of light entered that underground hole. I would sit silently, listening to my breath and heartbeats, until I couldn't take it anymore and then would race up the stairs and throw open the door. Light would avalanche into the cellar. What a change! Moments before I couldn't see anything—all of a sudden I could see everything.

Just as light poured into the cellar, God's hope pours into your world. Upon the sick, he shines the ray of healing. To the bereaved, he gives the promise of reunion. For the dying, he lit the flame of resurrection. To the confused, he offers the light of Scripture.

God gives hope.

Traveling Light

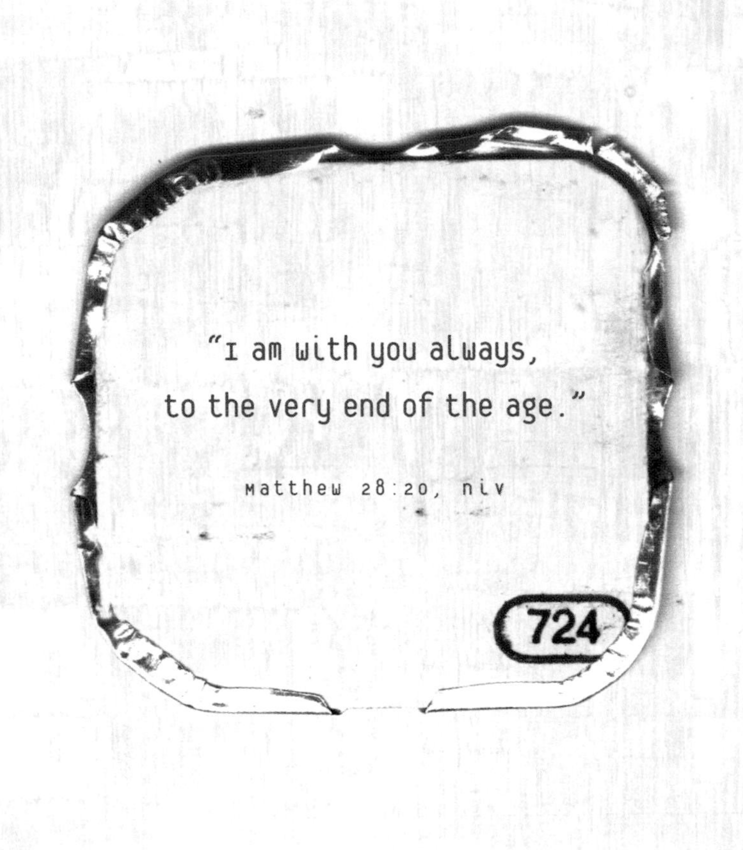

"I am with you always,
to the very end of the age."

Matthew 28:20, NIV

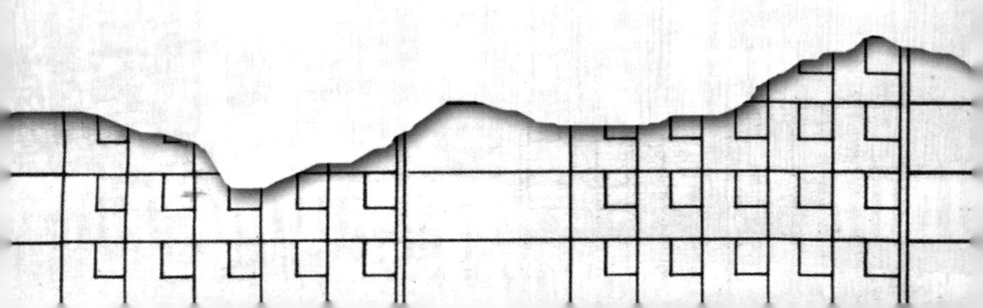

Love has hope in you.

The aspiring young author was in need of hope. More than one person had told him to give up. "Getting published is impossible," one mentor said. "Unless you are a national celebrity, publishers won't talk to you." Another warned, "Writing takes too much time. Besides, you don't want all your thoughts on paper."

Initially he listened. He agreed that writing was a waste of effort and turned his attention to other projects. But somehow the pen and pad were bourbon and Coke to the wordaholic. He'd rather write than read. So he wrote. How many nights did he pass on that couch in the corner of the apartment reshuffling his deck of verbs and nouns? And how many hours did his wife sit with him? He wordsmithing. She cross-stitching. Finally a manuscript was finished. Crude and laden with mistakes but finished.

She gave him the shove. "Send it out. What's the harm?"

So out it went. Mailed to fifteen different publishers. While the couple waited, he wrote. While he wrote, she stitched. Neither expecting much, both hoping everything. Responses began to fill the mailbox. "I'm sorry, but we don't accept unsolicited manuscripts." "We must return your work. Best of luck." "Our catalog doesn't have room for unpublished authors."

I still have those letters. Somewhere in a file. Finding them would take some time. Finding Denalyn's cross-stitch, however, would take none. To see it, all I do is lift my eyes from this monitor and look on the wall. "Of all those arts in which the wise excel, nature's chief masterpiece is writing well."

She gave it to me about the time the fifteenth letter arrived. A publisher had said yes. That letter is also framed. Which of the two is more meaningful? The gift from my wife or the letter from the publisher? The gift, hands down. For in giving the gift, Denalyn gave hope.

A Love Worth Giving

BOBBY PINS AND RUBBER BANDS

Your toughest challenge is nothing more than bobby pins and rubber bands to God. *Bobby pins and rubber bands?*

My older sister used to give them to me when I was a child. I would ride my tricycle up and down the sidewalk, pretending that the bobby pins were keys and my trike was a truck. But one day I lost the "keys." Crisis! What was I going to do? My search yielded nothing but tears and fear. But when I confessed my mistake to my sister, she just smiled. Being a decade older, she had a better perspective.

God has a better perspective as well. With all due respect, our severest struggles are, in his view, nothing worse than lost bobby pins and rubber bands. He is not confounded, confused, or discouraged.

Receive his hope, won't you? Receive it because you need it. Receive it so you can share it.

A Love Worth Giving

GOD RESTORES OUR HOPE

The story is told of a man on an African safari deep in the jungle. The guide before him had a machete and was whacking away the tall weeds and thick underbrush. The traveler, wearied and hot, asked in frustration, "Where are we? Do you know where you are taking me? Where is the path?!" The seasoned guide stopped and looked back at the man and replied, "I am the path."

We ask the same questions, don't we? We ask God, "Where are you taking me? Where is the path?" And he, like the guide, doesn't tell us. Oh, he may give us a hint or two, but that's all. If he did, would we understand? Would we comprehend our location? No, like the traveler, we are unacquainted with this jungle. So rather than give us an answer,

Jesus gives us a far greater gift. He gives us himself.

Does he remove the jungle? No, the vegetation is still thick.

Does he purge the predators? No, danger still lurks. Jesus doesn't give hope by changing the jungle; he restores our hope by giving us himself. And he has promised to stay until the very end.

Traveling Light

SECTION SEVEN

Looking at LIFE

POST CARD
THIS SIDE FOR THE ADDRESS
You need to learn a secret.
what you have in your shepherd
is greater than
what you don't have in life.

May I meddle for a moment? What is the one thing separating you from joy? How do you fill in this blank: "I will be happy when ____________"? When I am healed. When I am promoted. When I am married. When I am single. When I am rich. How would you finish that statement?

Now, with your answer firmly in mind, answer this. If your ship never comes in, if your dream never comes true, if the situation never changes, could you be happy? If not, then you are sleeping in the cold cell of discontent. You are in prison. And you need to know what you have in your Shepherd.

You have a God who hears you, the power of love behind you, the Holy Spirit within you, and all of heaven ahead of you. If you have the Shepherd, you have grace for every sin, direction for every turn, a candle for every corner, and an anchor for every storm. You have everything you need.

Traveling Light

The
Lord is my Shepherd;
I shall not want.
Psalm 23:1, NKJV

HE'S BEEN THERE

A couple of days ago twenty thousand of us ran through the streets of San Antonio, raising money for breast cancer research. Most of us ran out of kindness, happy to log three miles and donate a few dollars to the cause. A few ran in memory of a loved one, others in honor of a cancer survivor. We ran for different reasons. But no runner was more passionate than one I spotted. A bandanna covered her bald head, and dark circles shadowed her eyes. She had cancer. While we ran out of kindness, she ran out of conviction. She knows how cancer victims feel. She's been there.

The phrase "I've been there" is in the chorus of Christ's theme song. To the lonely, Jesus whispers, "I've been there." To the discouraged, Christ nods his head and sighs, "I've been there."

Jesus has been there. He experienced "all the pain, all the testing" (Hebrews 2:18, MSG). Jesus was angry enough to purge the temple, hungry enough to eat raw grain, distraught enough to weep in public, fun loving enough to be called a drunkard, winsome enough to attract kids, weary enough to sleep in a storm-bounced boat, poor enough to sleep on dirt and borrow a coin for a sermon illustration, radical enough to get kicked out of town, responsible enough to care for his mother, tempted enough to know the smell of Satan, and fearful enough to sweat blood.

Next Door Savior

but why?

why would heaven's finest son endure earth's toughest pain? so you would know that "he is able...to run to the cry of... those who are being tempted and tested and tried" (Hebrew 2:18, AMP).

whatever you are facing, he knows how you feel.

UNCOMMON COMMONALITIES

You awoke today to a common day. No butler drew your bath. No maid laid out your clothes. Your eggs weren't Benedict, and your orange juice wasn't fresh squeezed. But that's OK; there's nothing special about the day. It's not your birthday or Christmas; it's like every other day. A common day.

So you went to the garage and climbed into your common car. You once read that children of the queen never need to drive. You've been told of executives and sheiks who are helicoptered to their offices. As for you, a stretch limo took you to your wedding reception, but since then it's been sedans and minivans. Common cars.

Common cars that take you to your common job. You take it seriously, but you would never call it extraordinary. You're not clearing your calendar for Jay Leno or making time to appear before Congress. You're just making sure you get your work done before the six o'clock rush turns the Loop into a parking lot.

You lead a common life. Punctuated by occasional weddings, job transfers, bowling trophies, and graduations—a few highlights—but mainly the day-to-day rhythm that you share with the majority of humanity.

Jesus listened to his common life.

Are you listening to yours? Rain pattering against the window. Silent snow in April. The giggle of a baby on a crowded plane. Seeing a sunrise while the world sleeps. Are these not personal epistles? Can't God speak through a Monday commute or a midnight diaper change? Take notes on your life.

Next time your life feels ordinary, take your cue from Christ. Pay attention to your work and your world. Jesus' obedience began in a small town carpentry shop. His uncommon approach to his common life groomed him for his uncommon call.

Next Door Savior

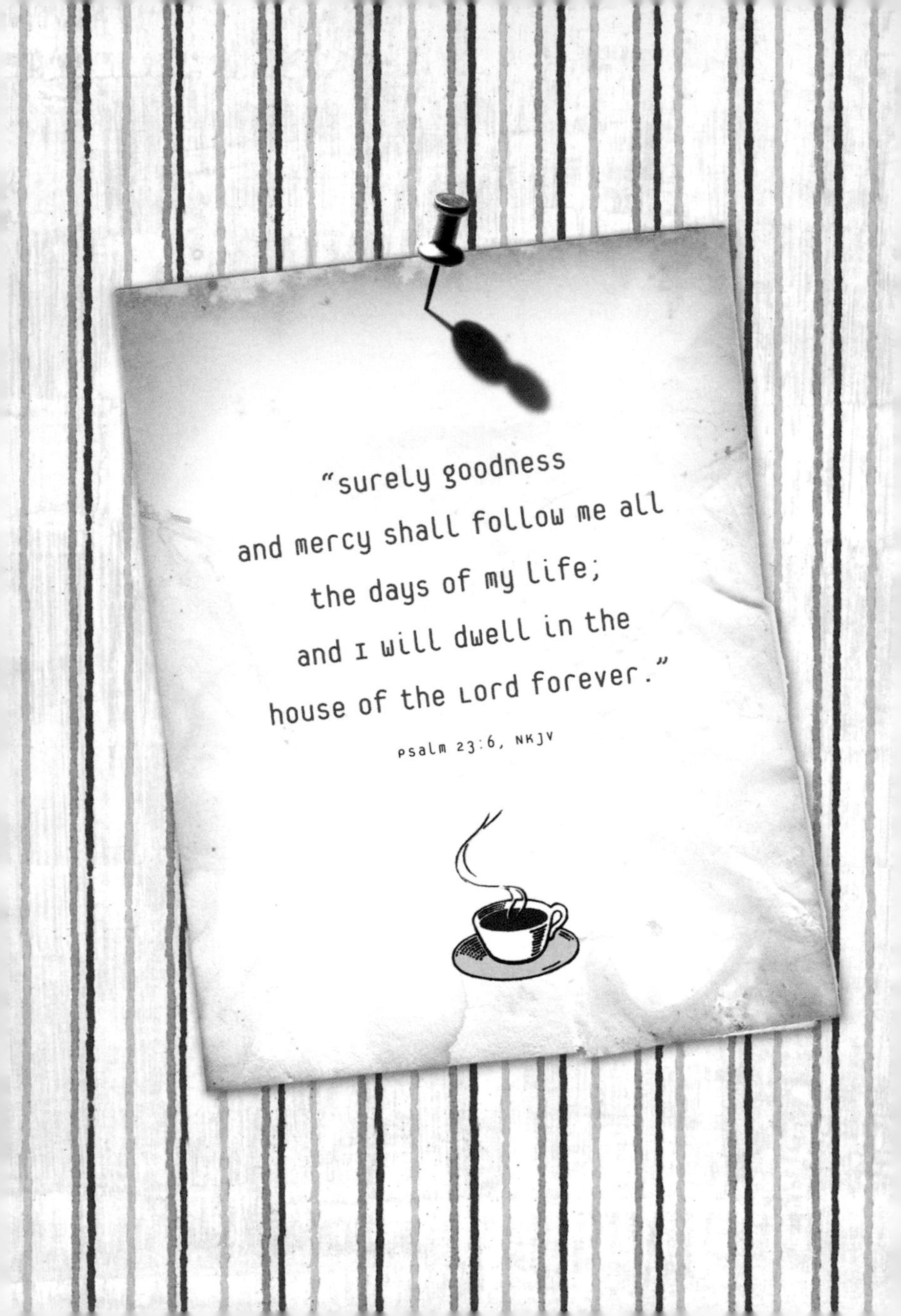
"surely goodness
and mercy shall follow me all
the days of my life;
and I will dwell in the
house of the Lord forever."
Psalm 23:6, NKJV

what a huge statement. Look at the size of it! Goodness and mercy follow the child of God each and every day! Think of the days that lie ahead. What do you see?

Days at home with only toddlers? God will be at your side.

Days in a dead-end job? He will walk you through.

Days of loneliness? He will take your hand.

Surely goodness and mercy shall follow me—not some, not most, not nearly all—but all the days of my life.

Traveling Light

God always rejoices when we dare to dream. In fact, we are much like God when we dream. The Master exults in newness. He delights in stretching the old. He wrote the book on making the impossible possible.

Examples? Check the Book.

Eighty-year-old shepherds don't usually play chicken with Pharaohs . . . but don't tell that to Moses.

Teenage shepherds don't normally have showdowns with giants . . . but don't tell that to David.

Night-shift shepherds don't usually get to hear angels sing and see God in a stable . . . but don't tell that to the Bethlehem bunch.

And for sure don't tell that to God.

And the Angels Were Silent

Jesus doesn't limit
his recruiting to the stout-hearted.
The beat up and worn out are
prime prospects in his book, and he's been
known to climb into boats, bars,
and brothels to tell them,
"It's not too late
to start over."

SECTION EIGHT
Life doesn't happen without
PAIN and TEARS.
Let's talk about that.

God **KNOWS** How You Feel...

A friend of mine was recently trying to teach his six-year-old son how to shoot a basket. The boy would take the basketball and push it as hard as he could toward the goal, but it always fell short. The father would then take the ball and toss it toward the basket, saying something like, "Just do it like this, son. It's easy."

Then the boy would try, and miss, again. My friend would then take the ball and make another basket, encouraging his son to push the ball a bit harder.

After several minutes and many misses, the boy responded to his father's encouragement by saying, "Yeah, but it's easy for you up there. You don't know how hard it is from down here."

You and I can never say that about God. Of the many messages Jesus taught us about stress, the first one is this: "God knows how you feel."

in the eye of the storm

what do you do

with a cup of disappointment?

Have you taken your disappointments to God? You've shared them with your neighbor, your relatives, your friends. But have you taken them to God? James says, "Anyone who is having troubles should pray" (James 5:13, NCV).

Before you go anywhere else with your disappointments, go to God.

Maybe you don't want to trouble God with your hurts. After all, he's got famines and pestilence and wars; he won't care about my little struggles, you think. Why don't you let him decide that? He cared enough about a wedding to provide the wine. He cared enough about Peter's tax payment to give him a coin. He cared enough about the woman at the well to give her answers. "He cares about you" (1 Peter 5:7, NCV).

Traveling Light

GOD WILL WIPE AWAY YOUR TEARS

When I was a young man, I had plenty of people to wipe away my tears. I had two big sisters who put me under their wings. I had a dozen or so aunts and uncles. I had a mother who worked nights as a nurse and days as a mother—excercising both professions with tenderness. I even had a brother three years my elder who felt sorry for me occasionally.

But when I think about someone wiping away my tears, I think about Dad. His hands were callused and tough, his fingers short and stubby. And when my father wiped away a tear, he seemed to wipe it away forever. There was something in his touch that took away more than the drop of hurt from my cheek. It also took away my fear.

John says that someday God will wipe away your tears. The same hands that stretched the heavens will touch your cheeks. The same hands that formed the mountains will caress your face. The same hands that curled in agony as the Roman spike cut through will someday cup your face and brush away your tears. Forever.

The Applause of Heaven

How did Jesus endure the terror of the crucifixion? He went first to the Father with his fears. He modeled the words of Psalm 56:3: "When I am afraid, I put my trust in you" (NLT).

"Father, if you are willing, take away this cup of suffering." The first one to hear his fear is his Father. He could have gone to his mother. He could have confided in his disciples. He could have assembled a prayer meeting. All would have been appropriate, but none were his priority. He went first to his Father.

Oh, how we tend to go everywhere else. First to the bar, to the counselor, to the self-help book or the friend next door. Not Jesus. The first one to hear his fear was his Father in heaven.

Traveling Light

POST CARD
THIS SIDE FOR THE ADDRESS
God's ways are always right.
They may not make sense to us.
They may be mysterious, inexplicable,
difficult, and even painful.
But they are right.

SEPTEMBER 11, 2001

On a September morning in 2001, Frank Silecchia laced up his boots, pulled on his hat, and headed out the door of his New Jersey house. As a construction worker, he made a living making things. But as a volunteer at the World Trade Center wreckage, he just tried to make sense of it all. He hoped to find a live body. He did not. He found forty-seven dead ones.

Amid the carnage, however, he stumbled upon a symbol—a twenty-foot-tall steel-beam cross. The collapse of Tower One on Building Six created a crude chamber in the clutter. In the chamber, through the dusty sunrise, Frank spotted the cross.

No winch had hoisted it; no cement secured it. The iron beams stood independent of human help. Standing alone, but not alone. Other crosses rested randomly at the base of the large one.

Different sizes, different angles, but all crosses.

Several days later engineers realized the beams of the large cross came from two different buildings. When one crashed into another, the two girders bonded into one, forged by the fire.

A symbol in the shards. A cross found in the crisis. "Where is God in all this?" we asked. The discovery dared us to hope, "Right in the middle of it all."

Next Door Savior

we can deal with the ambulance if God is in it.
we can stomach the ICU if God is in it.
we can face the empty house
if God is in it. He is.

God will
wipe away every tear
from their eyes.
Revelation 21:4, NKJV

LISTENING AND TRUSTING

On a trip to the United Kingdom, our family visited a castle. In the center of the garden sat a maze. Row after row of shoulder-high hedges, leading to one dead end after another. Successfully navigate the labyrinth, and discover the door to a tall tower in the center of the garden. Were you to look at our family pictures of the trip, you'd see four of our five family members standing on the top of the tower. Hmmm, someone is still on the ground. Guess who? I was stuck in the foliage. I just couldn't figure out which way to go.

Ah, but then I heard a voice from above. "Hey, Dad." I looked up to see Sara, peering through the turret at the top. "You're going the wrong way," she explained. "Back up and turn right."

Do you think I trusted her? I didn't have to. I could have trusted my own instincts, consulted other confused tourists, sat and pouted and wondered why God would let this happen to me. But do you know what I did? I listened. Her vantage point was better than mine. She was above the maze. She could see what I couldn't.

Don't you think we should do the same with God?

Next Door Savior

SECTION NINE
Try to treat PEOPLE
the way you want God to treat you.

Those whom the people called trash, Jesus called treasures.

JESUS WAS TOUCHABLE, approachable, reachable. And, what's more, he was ordinary. If he were here today you probably wouldn't notice him as he walked through a shopping mall. He wouldn't turn heads by the clothes he wore or the jewelry he flashed.

"Just call me Jesus," you can almost hear him say.

He was the kind of fellow you'd invite to watch the Rams–Giants game at your house. He'd wrestle on the floor with your kids, doze on your couch, and cook steaks on your grill. He'd laugh at your jokes and tell a few of his own. And when you spoke, he'd listen to you as if he had all the time in eternity.

And one thing's for sure, you'd invite him back.

GOD CAME NEAR

The humble heart

honors others.

Is Jesus not our example? Content to be known as a carpenter. Happy to be mistaken for the gardener. He served his followers by washing their feet. He serves us by doing the same. Each morning he gifts us with beauty. Each Sunday he calls us to his table. Each moment he dwells in our hearts. And does he not speak of the day when he as "the master will dress himself to serve and tell the servants to sit at the table, and he will serve them" (Luke 12:37, NCV)?

If Jesus is so willing to honor us, can we not do the same for others? Make people a priority. Accept your part in his plan. Be quick to share the applause. And, most of all, regard others as more important than yourself. Love does.

A Love Worth Giving

Love does not delight in evil but rejoices with the truth" (1 Corinthians 13:6, NIV). In this verse lies a test for love.

Here's an example. A classic one. A young couple are on a date. His affection goes beyond her comfort zone. She resists. But he tries to persuade her with the oldest line in the book: "But I love you. I just want to be near you. If you loved me . . ."

That siren you hear? It's the phony-love detector. This guy doesn't love her. He may love having sex with her. He may love her body. He may love boasting to his buddies about his conquest. But he doesn't love her. True love will never ask the "beloved" to do what he or she thinks is wrong.

Love doesn't tear down the convictions of others. Quite the contrary.

"Love builds up" (1 Corinthians 8:1, NIV).

Do you want to know if your love for someone is true? If your friendship is genuine? Ask yourself: Do I influence this person to do what is right?

A Love Worth Giving

HERE'S A QUIZ . . .

Now I see why powerful people often wear sunglasses—the spotlight blinds them to reality. They suffer from a delusion that power means something (it doesn't). They are under the impression that earthly authority will make a heavenly difference (it won't).

Can I prove my point? Take this quiz.

Name the ten wealthiest men in the world.

Name the last ten Heisman trophy winners.

Name the last ten winners of the Miss America contest.

Name eight people who have won the Nobel or Pulitzer prize.

How about the last ten Academy Award winners for best picture or the last decade's worth of World Series winners?

How did you do? I didn't do well either. Surprising how quickly we forget, isn't it? And these are the best in their fields. But the applause dies. Awards tarnish. Achievements are forgotten.

Here's another quiz. See how you do on this one.

Think of three people you enjoy spending time with.

Name ten people who have taught you something worthwhile.

Name five friends who have helped you in a difficult time.

List a few teachers who aided your journey through school.

Easier? It was for me, too. The lesson? The people who make a difference are not the ones with the credentials, but the ones with the concern.

and the angels were silent

It is best
to listen much,
speak little.
James 1:19, TLB

we tend to speak much and listen little. There is a time to speak. But there is also a time to be quiet. That's what my father did. Dropping a fly ball may not be a big deal to most people, but if you are thirteen years old and have aspirations of the big leagues, it is a big deal. Not only was it my second error of the game, it allowed the winning run to score.

I didn't even go back to the dugout. I turned around in the middle of left field and climbed over the fence. I was halfway home when my dad found me. He didn't say a word. Just pulled over to the side of the road, leaned across the seat, and opened the passenger door. We didn't speak. We didn't need to. We both knew the world had come to an end. When we got home, I went straight to my room, and he went straight to the kitchen. Presently he appeared in front of me with cookies and milk. He took a seat on the bed, and we broke bread together. Somewhere in the dunking of the cookies I began to realize that life and my father's love would go on. In the economy of male adolescence, if you love the guy who drops the ball, then you really love him. My skill as a baseball player didn't improve, but my confidence in Dad's love did. Dad never said a word. But he did show up. He did listen up.

A Love Worth Giving

Kind hearts are quietly kind.
They let the car cut into traffic
and the young mom with three kids
move up in the checkout line.
They pick up the neighbor's trash can
that rolled into the street.

SOME DAYS NEVER COME

"Someday, I can take her on the cruise."

"Someday, I will have time to call and chat."

"Someday, the children will understand why I was so busy."

But you know the truth, don't you? You know even before I write it. You could say it better than I.

Some days never come.

And the price of practicality is sometimes higher than extravagance.

But the rewards of risky love are always greater than its cost.

Go to the effort. Invest the time. Write the letter. Make the apology. Take the trip. Purchase the gift. Do it. The seized opportunity renders joy. The neglected brings regret.

And the Angels were Silent

There is only so much sand in the hourglass. Who gets it?

You know what I'm talking about, don't you?

"The PTA needs a new treasurer. With your background and experience and talent and wisdom and love for kids . . . YOU are the perfect one for the job!"

"I apologize that I have to ask you again, but you are such a good Sunday-school teacher."

"I just lost my hygienist. Will you come back to work for me?"

It's tug-of-war, and you are the rope.

On one side are the requests for your time and energy. They call. They compliment. They are valid and good. Great opportunities to do good things. If they were evil, it'd be easy to say no. But they aren't, so it's easy to rationalize.

On the other side are the loved ones in your world. They don't write letters. They don't ask you to consult your calendar. They don't offer to pay your expenses. They don't use terms like "appointment," "engagement," or "do lunch." They don't want you for what you can do for them; they want you for who you are.

In the Eye of the Storm

Once a week,
let a child take you on a walk.

Be doubly kind to the people
who bring your food or park your car.

Never miss a chance
to read a child a story.

SECTION TEN
Do you know about GOD'S
ETERNAL PLAN?

God's greatest creation
is his eternal plan
to reach his children.

when our oldest daughter, Jenna, was two, I lost her in a department store. One minute she was at my side and the next she was gone. I panicked. All of a sudden only one thing mattered—I had to find my daughter. Shopping was forgotten. The list of things I came to get was unimportant. I yelled her name. What people thought didn't matter. For a few minutes, every ounce of energy had one goal—to find my lost child. (I did, by the way. She was hiding behind some jackets!)

No price is too high for a parent to pay to redeem his child. No energy is too great. No effort too demanding. A parent will go to any length to find his or her own.

So will God.

Mark it down. God's greatest creation is not the flung stars or the gorged canyons; it's his eternal plan to reach his children.

And the Angels Were Silent

Christ Jesus . . . ,
being in very nature God,
did not consider equality with God
something to be grasped,
but made himself nothing, taking the
very nature of a servant,
being made in human likeness.
And being found in appearance as a man,
he humbled himself and
became obedient to death—
even death on a cross!
Philippians 2:5-8, NIV

IF YOU WERE GOD, would you sleep on straw, nurse from a breast, and be clothed in a diaper? I wouldn't, but Christ did.

If you knew that only a few would care that you came, would you still come? If you knew that the tongues you made would mock you, the mouths you made would spit at you, the hands you made would crucify you, would you still make them? Christ did. Would you regard the immobile and invalid more important than yourself? Jesus did.

He humbled himself. He went from commanding angels to sleeping in the straw. From holding stars to clutching Mary's finger. The palm that held the universe took the nail of a soldier.

Why? Because that's what love does. It puts the beloved before itself. Your soul was more important than his blood. Your eternal life was more important than his earthly life. Your place in heaven was more important to him than his place in heaven, so he gave up his so you could have yours.

He loves you that much.

A Love Worth Giving

The path to the cross tells us exactly how far God will go to call us back.

CHRIST PAID OUR DEBT

Jesus did for us what I did for one of my daughters in the shop at New York's La Guardia Airport. The sign above the ceramic pieces read Do Not Touch. But the wanting was stronger than the warning, and she touched. And it fell. By the time I looked up, ten-year-old Sara was holding the two pieces of a New York City skyline. Next to her was an unhappy store manager. Over them both was the written rule. Between them hung a nervous silence. My daughter had no money. The manager had no mercy. So I did what dads do. I stepped in. "How much do *we* owe you?" I asked.

How was it that I owed anything? Simple. She was my daughter. And since she could not pay, I did.

Since you and I cannot pay, Christ did. We've

broken so much more than souvenirs. We've broken commandments, promises, and, worst of all, we've broken God's heart.

But Christ sees our plight. With the law on the wall and shattered commandments on the floor, he steps near (like a neighbor) and offers a gift (like a Savior).

What do we owe? We owe God a perfect life. Perfect obedience to every command. Not just the command of baptism, but the commands of humility, honesty, integrity. We can't deliver. Might as well charge us for the property of Manhattan. But Christ can and he did.

Next Door Savior

For God so loved
the world
That he gave his
only Son.
John 3:16, NLT

HOW WIDE HIS LOVE

As boldly as the center beam of the cross proclaims God's holiness, the crossbeam declares his love. And, oh, how wide his love reaches.

Aren't you glad the verse does not read:

"For God so loved the rich . . . "?

Or, "For God so loved the famous . . . "?

Or, "For God so loved the thin . . . "?

It doesn't. Nor does it state, "For God so loved the Europeans or Africans . . . " "the sober or successful . . . " "the young or the old . . . "

No, when we read John 3:16, we simply (and happily) read, "For God so loved the world."

How wide is God's love? Wide enough for the whole world. Are you included in the world? Then you are included in God's love.

He chose the Nails

JOE ALLBRIGHT is a fair and fearless West Texas rancher, a square-jawed, rawboned man with a neck by Rawlings. In Andrews County, where I was raised, everyone knew him.

One of Joe's sons, James, and I were best friends in high school. We played football together. (More honest, he played while I guarded the team bench.) One Friday night after an out-of-town game, James invited me to stay at his house. By the time we reached his property, the hour was way past midnight, and he hadn't told his father he was bringing anyone home.

Mr. Allbright didn't know me or my vehicle, so when I stepped out of the car in front of his house, he popped on a floodlight and aimed it right at my face. Through the glare I saw this block of a man (I think he was in his underwear), and I heard his deep voice. "Who are you?" I gulped. My mind moved at the speed of cold honey. I started to say my name but didn't. *Mr. Allbright doesn't know me.* My only hope was that James would speak up. A glacier could have melted before he did so.

Finally he interceded. "It's okay, Dad. That's my friend Max. He's with me." The light went off, and Mr. Allbright threw open the door. "Come on in, boys. Food is in the kitchen."

What changed? What made Mr. Allbright flip off the light? One fact. I had aligned myself with his son. My sudden safety had nothing to do with my accomplishments or offerings. I knew his son. Period.

For the same reason, you need never fear God's judgment. Not today. Not on Judgment Day. Jesus, in the light of God's glory, is speaking on your behalf. "That's my friend," he says. And when he does, the door of heaven opens.

come Thirsty

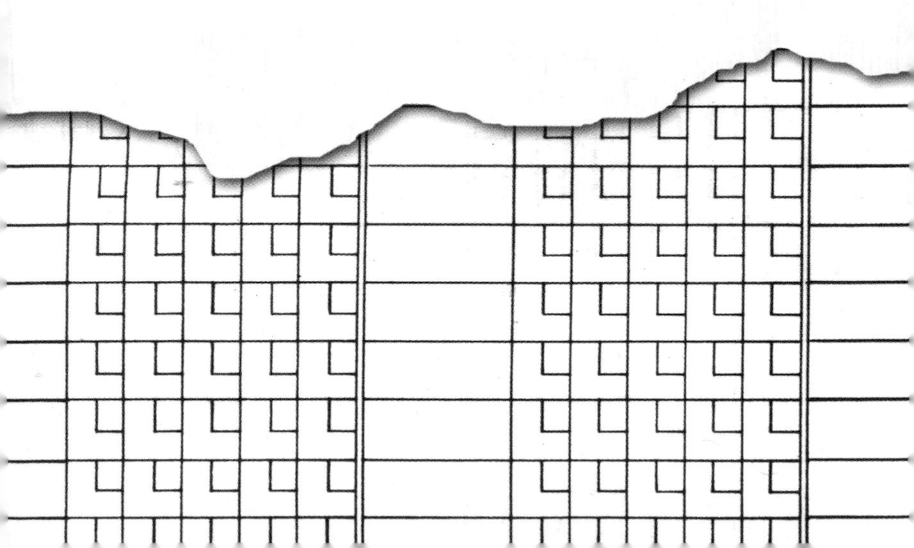

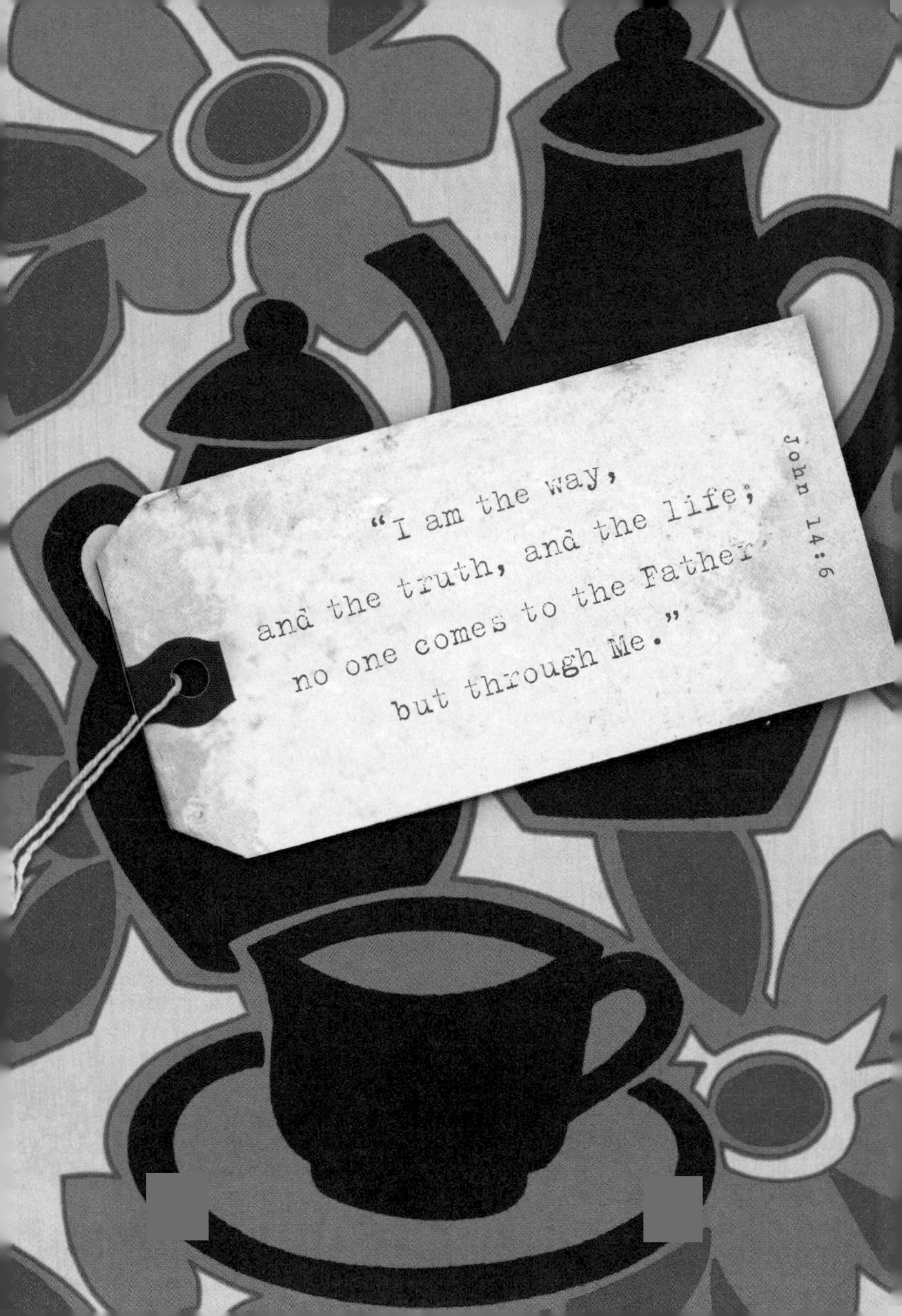
"I am the way,
and the truth, and the life;
no one comes to the Father
but through Me."
John 14:6

Make no mistake, Jesus saw himself as God. He leaves us with two options. Accept him as God, or reject him as a megalomaniac. There is no third alternative.

Oh, but we try to create one. Suppose I did the same? Suppose you came across me standing on the side of the road. I can go north or south. You ask me which way I'm going. My reply? "I'm going sorth."

Thinking you didn't hear correctly, you ask me to repeat the answer.

"I'm going sorth. I can't choose between north and south, so I'm going both. I'm going sorth."

"You can't do that," you reply. "You have to choose."

"OK," I concede, "I'll head nouth."

"Nouth is not an option!" you insist. "It's either north or south. One way or the other. To the right or to the left. When it comes to this road, you gotta pick."

When it comes to Christ, you've got to do the same. Call him crazy, or crown him as king. Dismiss him as a fraud, or declare him to be God. Walk away from him, or bow before him, but don't play games with him. Don't call him a great man. Don't list him among decent folk. Don't clump him with Moses, Elijah, Buddha, Joseph Smith, Muhammad, or Confucius. He didn't leave that option. He is either God or godless. Heaven sent or hell born. All hope or all hype. But nothing in between.

Next Door Savior

The definitive voice
in the universe is Jesus.
He is not one among many voices;
he is the one voice over all voices.

I grew up playing football in the empty field next to our house. Many a Sunday afternoon was spent imitating Don Meredith or Bob Hayes or Johnny Unitas. (Didn't have to imitate Joe Namath. Most of the girls thought I looked like him already.)

Empty fields in West Texas have grass burrs. Grass burrs hurt. You can't play football without falling, and you can't fall in a West Texas field without getting stuck.

More times than I can remember I pulled myself out of a sticker patch so hopelessly covered that I had to have help. Kids don't rely on other kids to pull out grass burrs. You need someone with skill. I would limp to the house so my dad could pluck out the stickers—one by painful one.

I wasn't too bright, but I knew this: If I wanted to get back into the game, I needed to get rid of those stickers.

Every mistake in life is like a grass burr. You

can't live without falling, and you can't fall without getting stuck. But guess what? We aren't always as smart as young ballplayers. We sometimes try to get back into the game without dealing with the stickers. It's as if we don't want anyone to know we fell, so we pretend we never did. Consequently, we live in pain. We can't walk well, sleep well, rest well. And, oh, are we touchy.

Does God want us to live like that? No way. Listen to his promise: "This is my commitment to my people: removal of their sins" (Rom. 11:27 MSG).

God does more than forgive our mistakes; he removes them! We simply have to take them to him.

He chose the Nails

"I will remember their sins no more."

Hebrews 8:12, RSV

SECTION ELEVEN

How do you simplify FAITH?...

...e has drawn near. He has involved
himself in the car pools, heartbreaks,
and funeral homes of our day. He is
as near to us on Monday as on Sunday.
In the scho[illegible]m as in the sanctuary.
At the coff[illegible] much as the
communion table.

He who receives Me
receives Him who sent Me.

Matthew 10:40, NCV

0120

simplify your faith by seeking God for yourself. No confusing ceremonies necessary. No mysterious rituals required. No elaborate channels of command or levels of access.

You have a Bible? You can study.

You have a heart? You can pray.

You have a mind. You can think.

just like jesus

Every morning
I tell you what I need,
and I wait for your answer.

PSALM 5:3, NCV

Before you face the day, face the Father. Before you step out of bed, step into his presence. I have a friend who makes it a habit to roll out of his bed onto his knees and begin his day in prayer. Personally, I don't get that far. With my head still on the pillow and my eyes still closed, I offer God the first seconds of my day. The prayer is not lengthy and far from formal. Depending on how much sleep I got, it may not even be intelligible. Often it's nothing more than "Thank you for a night's rest. I belong to you today."

JUST LIKE JESUS

A DEFINITION OF PRAYER

"Pray at all times and on every occasion," (Ephesians 6:18, NLT). Sound burdensome? Are you wondering, *My business needs attention, my children need dinner, my bills need paying. How can I stay in a place of prayer?* Unceasing prayer may sound complicated, but it needn't be that way.

Do this. Change your definition of prayer. Think of prayers less as an activity for God and more as an awareness of God. Seek to live in uninterrupted awareness. Acknowledge his presence everywhere you go. As you stand in line to register your car, think, *Thank you, Lord, for being here.* In the grocery as you shop, *Your presence, my King, I welcome.* As you wash the dishes, worship your Maker.

come Thirsty

pray at all times
and on every occasion.
ephesians 6:18, NLT
724

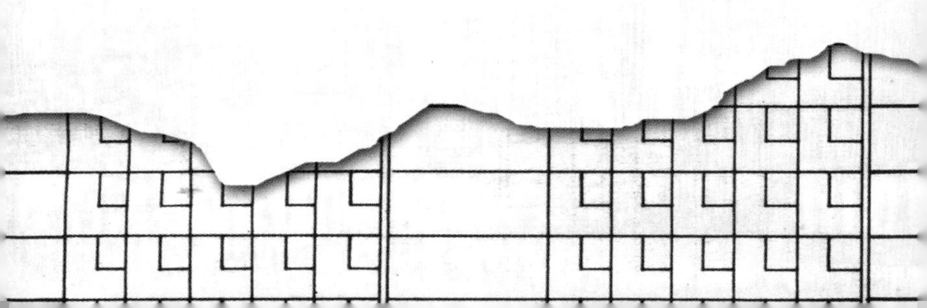

"Come to Me,
all you who labor and are heavy laden,
and I will give you rest.
Take My yoke upon you and learn from Me,
for I am gentle and lowly in heart,
and you will find rest for your souls.
For My yoke is easy
and My burden is light."

Matthew 11:28-30, NKJV

FARMERS IN ANCIENT ISRAEL used to train an inexperienced ox by yoking it to an experienced one with a wooden harness. The straps around the older animal were tightly drawn. He carried the load. But the yoke around the younger animal was loose. He walked alongside the more mature ox, but his burden was light. In this verse Jesus is saying, "I walk alongside you. We are yoked together. But I pull the weight and carry the burden."

I wonder, how many burdens is Jesus carrying for us that we know nothing about? We're aware of some. He carries our sin. He carries our shame. He carries our eternal debt. But are there others? Has he lifted fears before we felt them? Has he carried our confusion so we wouldn't have to? Those times when we have been surprised by our own sense of peace? Could it be that Jesus has lifted our anxiety onto his shoulders and placed a yoke of kindness on ours?

And how often do we thank him for his kindness? Not often enough.

A Love Worth Giving

when no one is watching,
live as if SOMEONE is.

LEARNING TO LISTEN TO GOD

A friend of mine married an opera soprano. She loves concerts. Her college years were spent in the music department, and her earliest memories are of keyboards and choir risers. He, on the other hand, leans more toward Monday Night Football and country music. He also loves his wife, so on occasion he attends an opera. The two sit side by side in the same auditorium, listening to the same music, with two completely different responses. He sleeps and she weeps.

I believe the difference is more than taste. It's training. She has spent hours learning to appreciate the art of music. He has spent none. Her ears are Geiger-counter sensitive. He can't differentiate between *staccato* and *legato.* But he is trying.

Last time we talked about the concerts, he told me he is managing to stay awake. He may never have the same ear as his wife, but with time he is learning to listen and appreciate the music.

I believe we can, too. Equipped with the right tools, we can learn to listen to God. What are those tools? Here are the ones I have found helpful:

A regular time and place.

An open Bible.

A listening heart.

Just Like Jesus

"Be careful what you think, because your thoughts run your life" (Proverbs 4:23, NCV).

What a true statement! Test the principle, and see if you don't agree.

Two drivers are stuck in the same traffic jam. One person stews in anger, thinking, *My schedule is messed up.* The other sighs in relief, *Good chance to slow down.*

Two mothers face the same tragedy. One is destroyed: *I'll never get over this.* The other is despondent but determined: *God will get me through.*

Two executives face the same success. One pats himself on the back and grows cocky. The other gives the credit to God and grows grateful.

Just Like Jesus

you've got to admit some of our hearts are trashed out. Let any riffraff knock on the door, and we throw it open. Anger shows up, and we let him in. Revenge needs a place to stay, so we have him pull up a chair. Pity wants to have a party, so we show him the kitchen. Lust rings the bell, and we change the sheets on the bed. Don't we know how to say no?

Many don't. For most of us, thought management is, well, unthought of. We think much about time management, weight management, personnel management, even scalp management. But what about thought management? Shouldn't we be as concerned about managing our thoughts as we are managing anything else?

just like jesus

"Thought management."
Now that's an interesting thought!

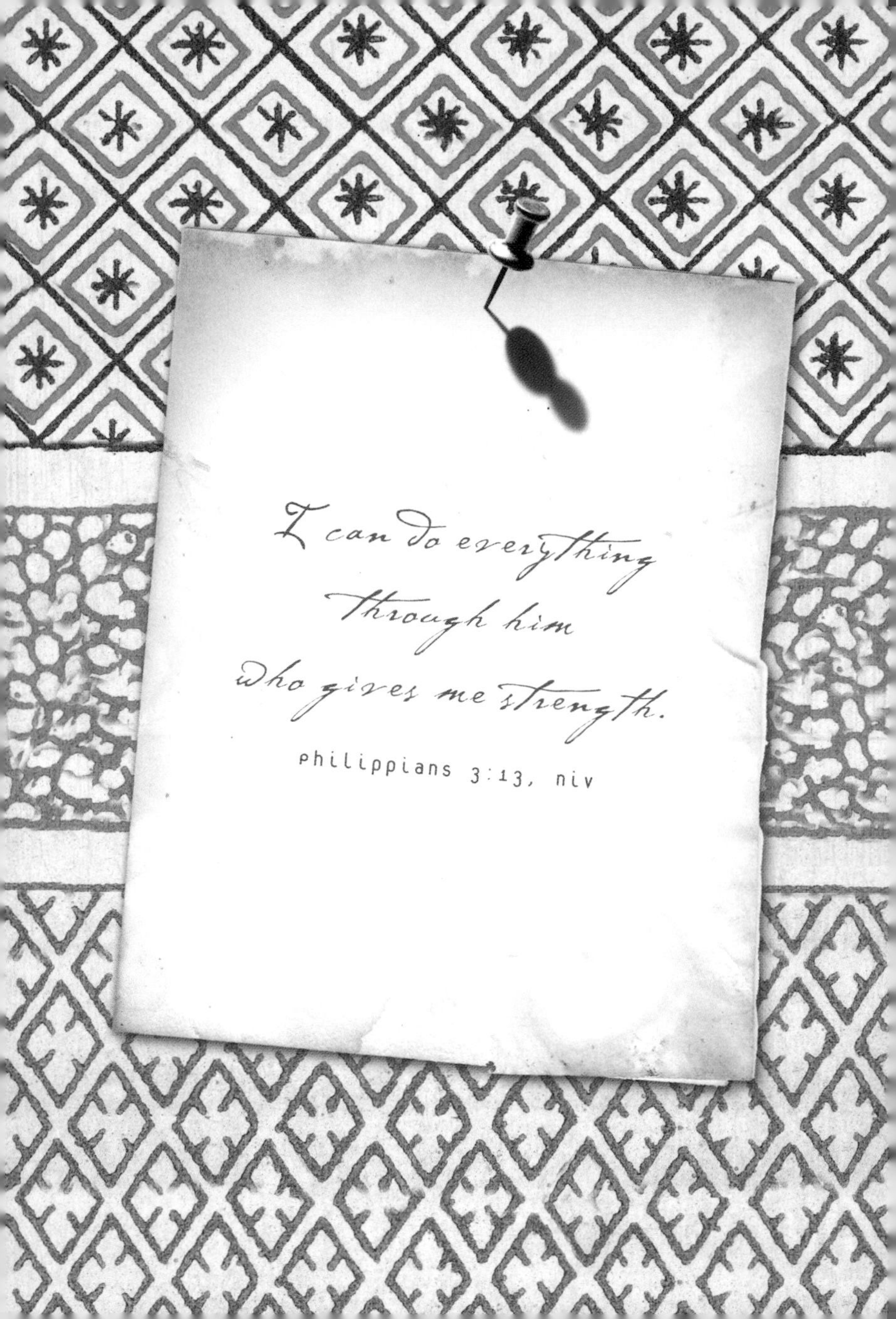
I can do everything
through him
who gives me strength.
philippians 3:13, niv

A MILLION IN YOUR ACCOUNT

God was *with* Adam and Eve, walking with them in the cool of the evening.

God was *with* Abraham, even calling the patriarch his friend.

God was *with* Moses and the children of Israel. Parents could point their children to the fire by night and cloud by day; *God is with us,* they could assure.

He was *with* the apostles. Peter could touch God's beard. John could watch God sleep. Multitudes could hear his voice. God was *with* them!

But he is *in* you. He will do what you cannot.

Imagine a million dollars being deposited into your checking account. To any observer you look the same, except for the goofy smile, but are you? Not at all! With God *in* you, you have a million resources that you did not have before!

Can't stop drinking? Christ can. And he lives within you.

Can't stop worrying? Christ can. And he lives within you.

Can't forgive the jerk, forget the past, or forsake your bad habits? Christ can! And he lives within you.

Next Door Savior

There is never a **nonsacred** moment! . . .

For years I viewed God as a compassionate CEO and my role as a loyal sales representative. He had his office, and I had my territory. I could contact him as much as I wanted. He was always a phone or fax away. He encouraged me, rallied behind me, and supported me, but he didn't go with me. At least I didn't think he did. Then I read 2 Corinthians 6:1: We are "God's fellow workers" (NIV).

Fellow workers? Co-laborers? God and I work together? Imagine the paradigm shift this truth creates. Rather than report to God, we work *with* God. Rather than check in with him and then leave, we check in with him and then follow. We are always in the presence of God. . . . There is never a nonsacred moment!

just like jesus

No one has ever imagined what God has prepared for those who love him.

1 Corinthians 2:9, NCV

Try this. Imagine a perfect world. Whatever that means to you, imagine it. Does that mean peace? Then envision absolute tranquility. Does a perfect world imply joy? Then create your highest happiness. Will a perfect world have love? If so ponder a place where love has no bounds. Whatever heaven means to you, imagine it. Get it firmly fixed in your mind. Delight in it. Dream about it. Long for it.

And then smile as the Father reminds you, *No one has ever imagined what God has prepared for those who love him.*

When it comes to describing heaven, we are all happy failures.

When God Whispers Your Name

we know
that when christ comes,
we will be like him,
because we will see him
as he really is.
1 John 3:2 , NCV

when you arrive in heaven . . . something wonderful will happen. A final transformation will occur. You will be just like Jesus.

Of all the blessings of heaven, one of the greatest will be you! You will be God's magnum opus, his work of art. The angels will gasp. God's work will be completed. At last, you will have a heart like his.

You will love with a perfect love.

You will worship with a radiant face.

You'll hear each word God speaks.

Your heart will be pure, your words will be like jewels, your thoughts will be like treasures.

You will be just like Jesus. You will, at long last, have a heart like his.

just like jesus

ACKNOWLEDGMENTS

Grateful acknowledgment is made to the following publishers for permission to reprint this copyrighted material. All copyrights are held by the author, Max Lucado.

And the Angels Were Silent (Nashville: W Publishing Group, 2003).

The Applause of Heaven (Nashville: W Publishing Group, 1990).

Come Thirsty (Nashville: W Publishing Group, 2004).

He Chose the Nails (Nashville: W Publishing Group, 2000).

God Came Near (Nashville: W Publishing Group, 2003).

In the Eye of the Storm (Nashville: W Publishing Group, 1991).

In the Grip of Grace (Nashville: W Publishing Group, 1996).

Just Like Jesus (Nashville: W Publishing Group, 1998).

A Love Worth Giving (Nashville: W Publishing Group, 2002).

Next Door Savior (Nashville: W Publishing Group, 2003).

Traveling Light (Nashville: W Publishing Group, 2000).

When God Whispers Your Name (Nashville: W Publishing Group, 1994).